ESSENTIAL GUITAR COLLECTION

CONTENTS

Cover photography: © Doors Photo Archives

ISBN 0-634-00214-7

HAL•LEONARD®
CORPORATION
7777 W. BLUEMOUND RD. P.O. BOX 13819 MILWAUKEE, WI 53213

Visit Hal Leonard Online at
www.halleonard.com

Photography by Henry Diltz

Back Door Man

Written by Willie Dixon

* Key signature denotes A Mixolydian.
** Chord symbols reflect implied tonality.

Verse

Gtr. 1: w/ Fill 1, 2nd time

2. And all you peo - ple they're try - 'n to sleep, _____ a yeah, I'm a back door _____ man. I'm out there mak - in' with my

Gtr. 1: w/ Fill 2, 2nd time

mid - night creep. _____ Yeah, _____ I'm a back door _____ 'cause I'm a back door

Fill 1
Gtr. 1

Fill 2
Gtr. 1

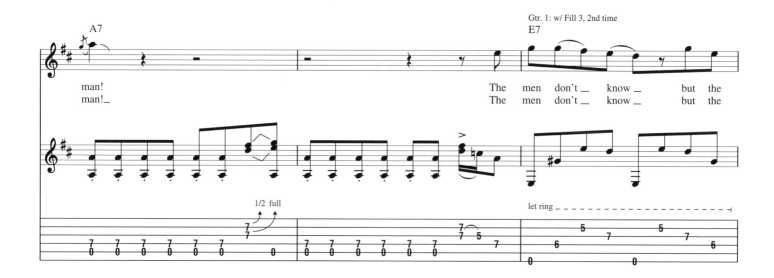

man!
man!

The men don't ___ know ___ but the
The men don't ___ know ___ but the

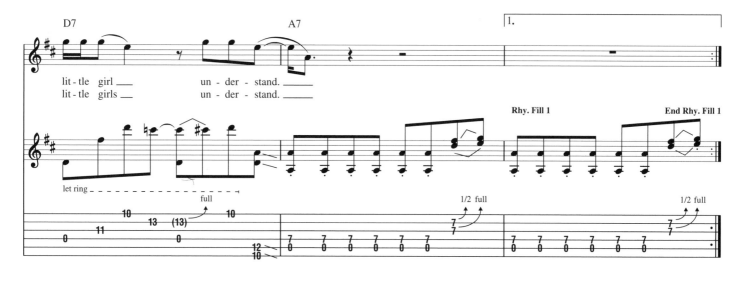

lit - tle girl ___ un - der - stand. _____
lit - tle girls ___ un - der - stand. _____

1.

Rhy. Fill 1   End Rhy. Fill 1

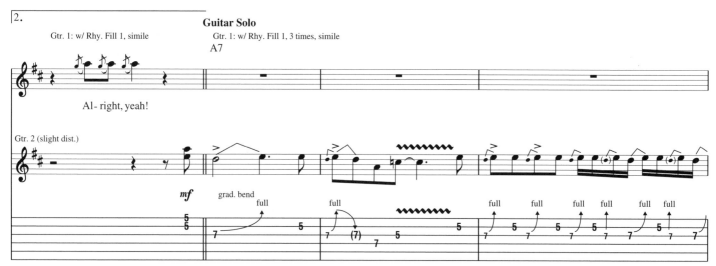

2.

Guitar Solo

Al - right, yeah!

Fill 3

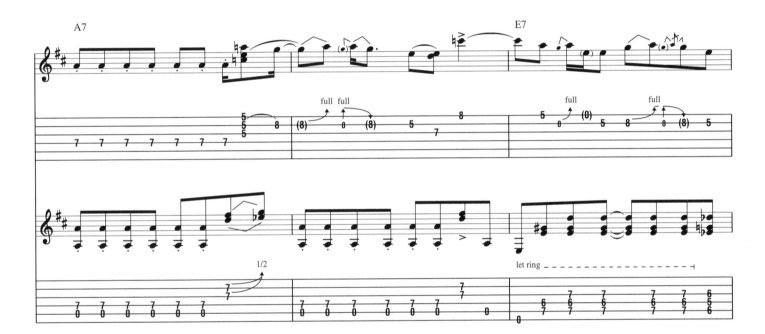

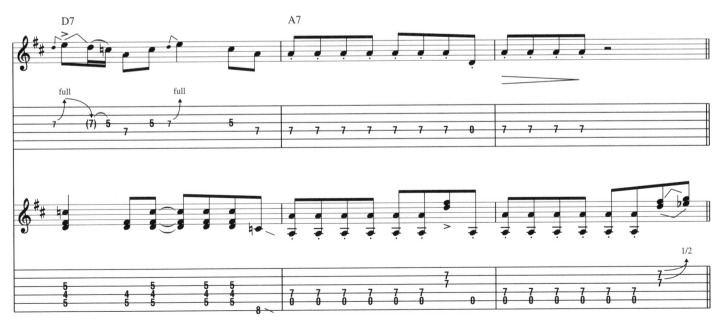

Interlude

Gtr. 2 tacet

Verse

3. You men eat your din-ner, eat your __ pork and beans. __ I eat more chick - en an - y

man ev - er seen. __ Yeah, __ yeah. __ I'm a back door __ man, wah.

The men don't __ know __ but the lit - tle girls __ un - der - stand. __

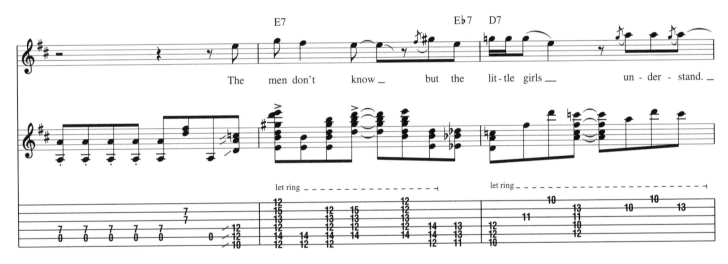

Break On Through (To the Other Side)

Words and Music by The Doors

Chorus

N.C.(Em)

Break on through _ to the oth - er side. _____ Break on through _ to the

To Coda ⊕ |1.

Interlude

N.C.(Em)

oth - er side. _ Break on through _ to the oth - er side, _ yeah.

|2.

2. We

P.M. ⌐

Organ Solo

w/ Lead Voc. ad lib
Gtr. 1: w/ Riff A, 8 times, simile

Bridge

Gtr. 1: w/ Riff A, 4 times, simile
N.C.(Em)

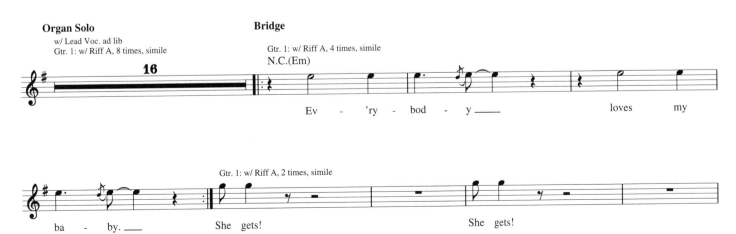

Ev - 'ry - bod - y ___ loves my

Gtr. 1: w/ Riff A, 2 times, simile

ba - by. ___ She gets! She gets!

She get! She get! Yeah.

D.S. al Coda

3. I found an

⊕ *Coda*

Break on through, __ oh! __ Oh, yeah! __

Verse

4. Made the scene __ week to week, __ day to day, __

* mute strings with right hand

Outro-Chorus

Gtr. 1: w/ Riff B

N.C.(Em)

Break on through _ to the oth - er side. _ Break on through _ to the oth - er side. _____

Break on through. _ Break on through. _ Break on through. _

Gtr. 1

Break on through. _ Heh, heh, eh, eh,

eh, eh, eh, eh, eh.

Hello, I Love You
(Won't You Tell Me Your Name?)

Words and Music by The Doors

* Key signature denotes A Mixolydian.
** Chord symbols reflect overall tonality.

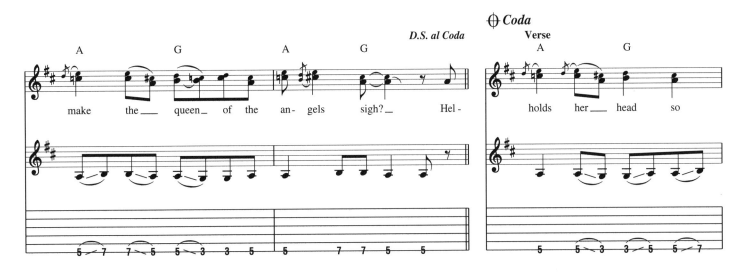

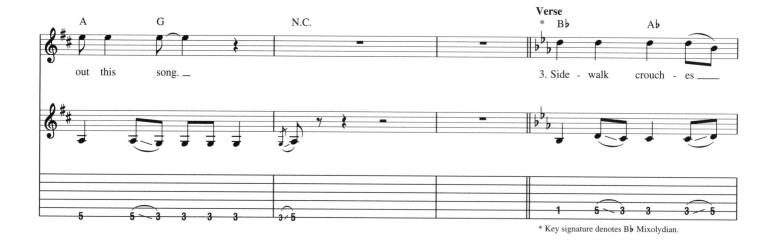

out this song. ___   3. Side - walk crouch - es ___

* Key signature denotes B♭ Mixolydian.

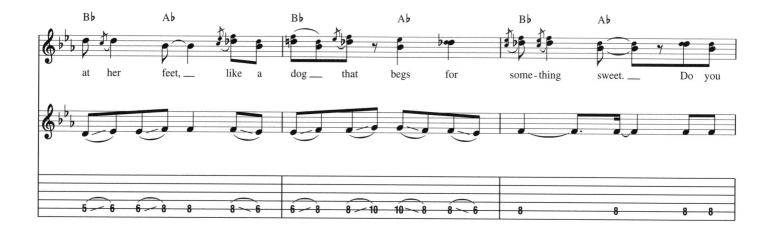

at her feet, ___ like a dog ___ that begs for some - thing sweet. ___ Do you

hope to ___ make her see you, fool? ___ Do you hope to pluck this

dus - ky jew - el?   Hel - lo!   Hel - lo!   Hel - lo!

Gtrs. 1 & 2 (dist.)

(Gtr. 2 cont. in slash)

L.A. Woman

Words and Music by The Doors

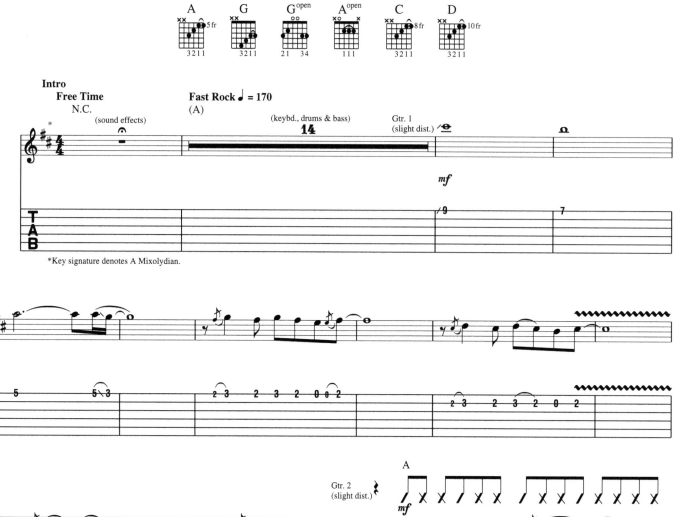

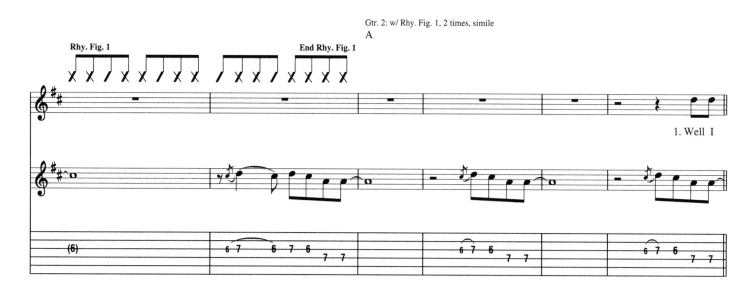

*Key signature denotes A Mixolydian.

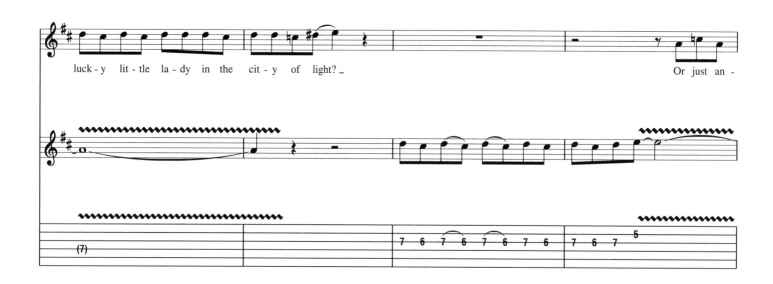

luck - y lit - tle la - dy in the cit - y of light? __ Or just an -

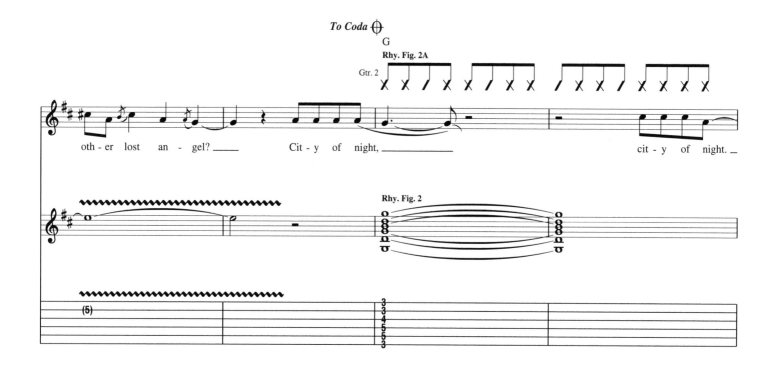

oth - er lost an - gel? __ Cit - y of night, __ cit - y of night. _

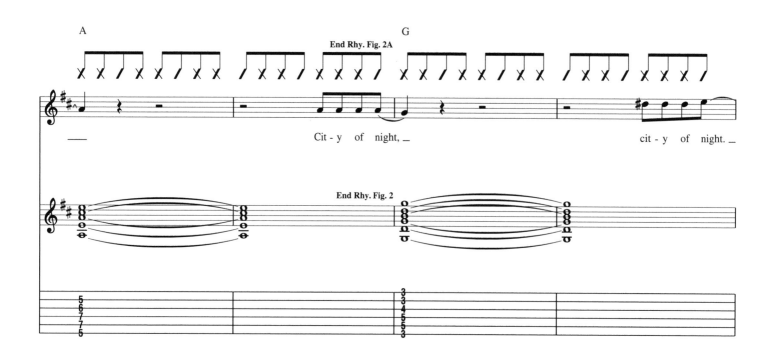

— Cit - y of night, _ cit - y of night. _

Whoa!   Come on!

Verse

Gtr. 2: w/ Rhy. Fig. 1, 8 times, simile

2. L. A. — wom - an,   L. A. — wom - an.

L. A. wom - an Sun-day af - ter - noon. —

L. A. wom - an Sun-day af - ter - noon. —

Gtrs. 1 & 2: w/ Rhy. Figs. 2 & 2A, 2 times, simile

In - to your blues. __ In - to your blues. __ Yeah! In - to your

blue, blue, __ blue, in - to your blues. Oh, __

Piano Solo
Gtr. 2: w/ Rhy. Fig. 1, 8 times, simile

yeah!

Interlude

Riff A
Gtrs. 1 & 2

let ring throughout

End Riff A
play 3 times

Bridge
Gtr. 1: w/ Riff A, 4 times
Gtr. 2: w/ Riff A, 8 times

see your hair is burn - ing, __

top-less bars, ___ nev - er saw a wom - an ___ so a -

Gtrs. 1 & 2: w/ Rhy. Figs. 2 & 2A, 2 times, simile

G   **A**

lone,   so a - lone. ___   So a -

G   **A**

lone,   so a - lone. ___

Gtr. 2: w/ Rhy. Fig. 1, 4 times, simile

Mo - tel mon - ey,   mur - der mad - ness,

Gtr. 1

a, change the mood from glad ___ to sad - ness.

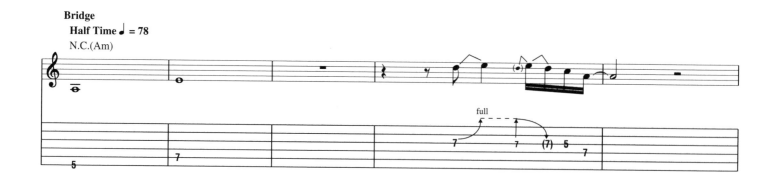

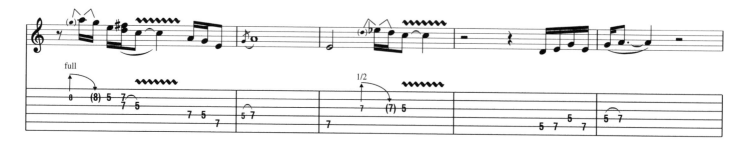

Yeah. _____

(cont. in slash)

Gtr. 2: w/ Rhy. Fig. 1, 2 times, simile

D.S. al Coda

3. Well,

L. A.   Wom - an. _____ You're my wom - an. _____ My lit - tle

L. A.   Wom - an. _____ Yeah, my L. A.   Wom - an, _____

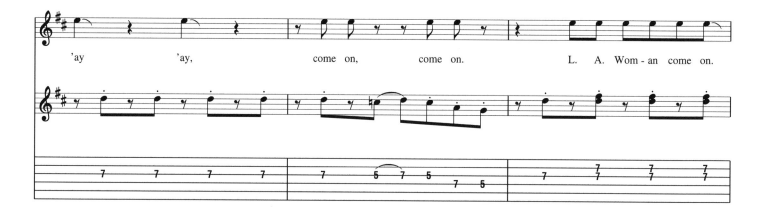

'ay   'ay,   come on,   come on.   L. A. Wom - an come on.

Begin Fade

Fade Out

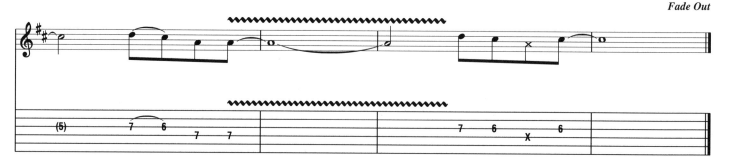

Light My Fire

Words and Music by The Doors

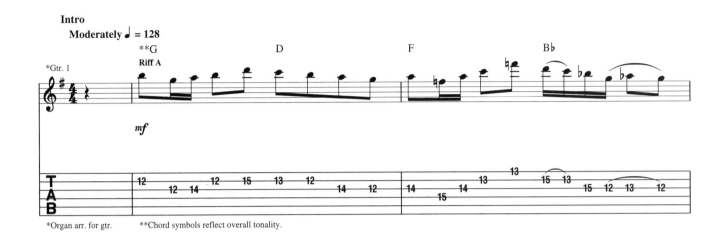

*Organ arr. for gtr.   **Chord symbols reflect overall tonality.

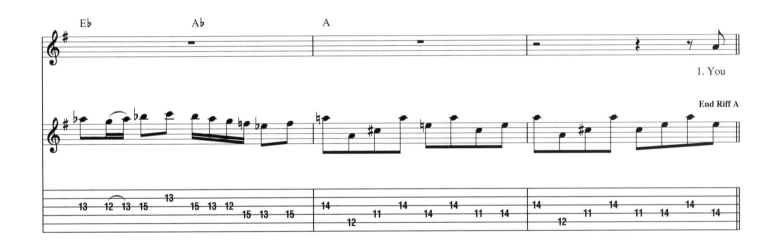

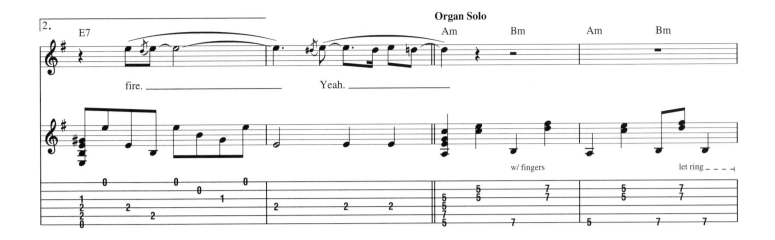

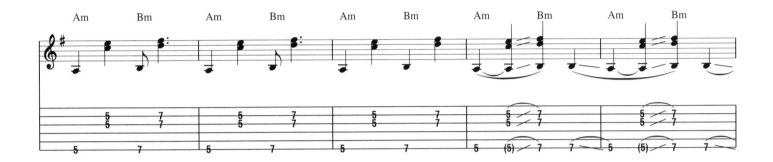

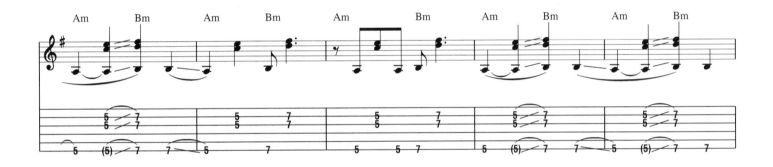

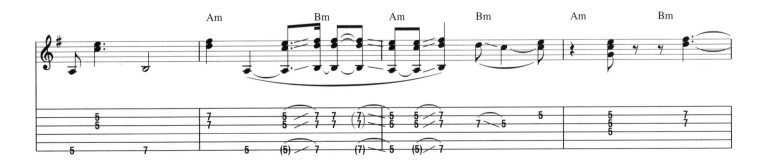

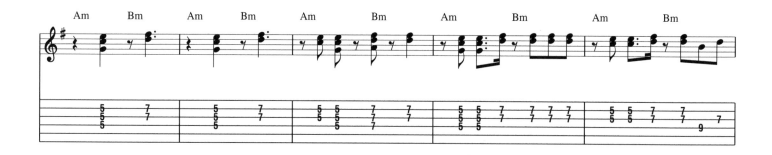

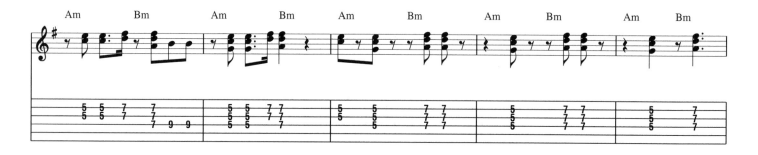

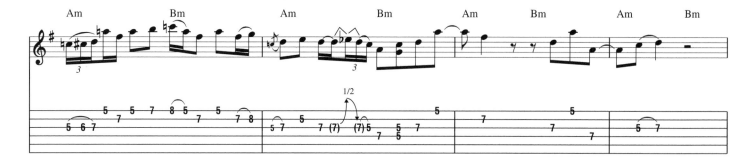

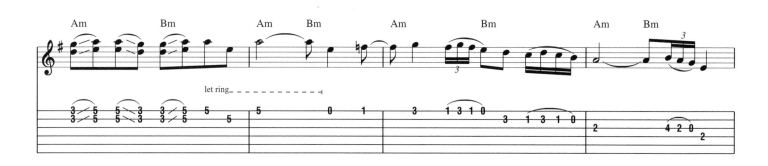

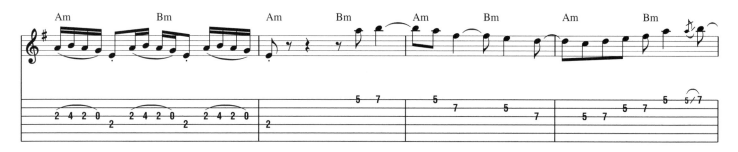

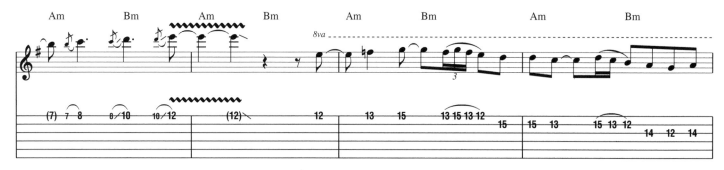

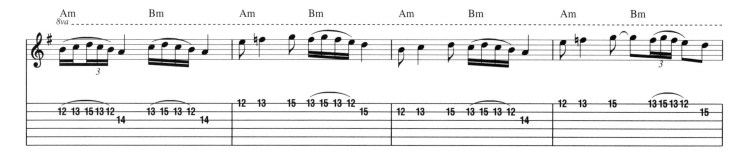

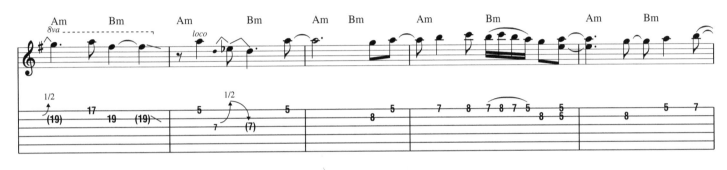

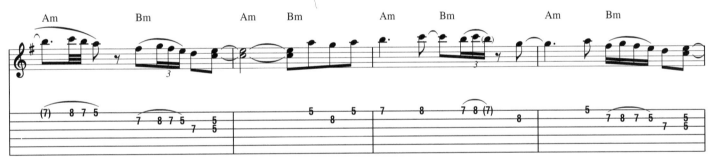

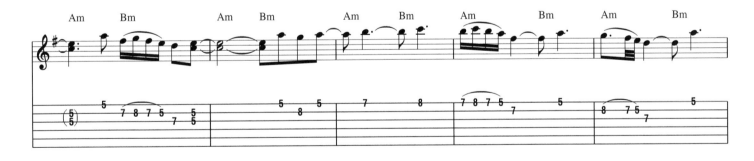

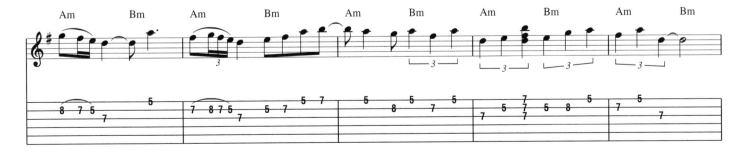

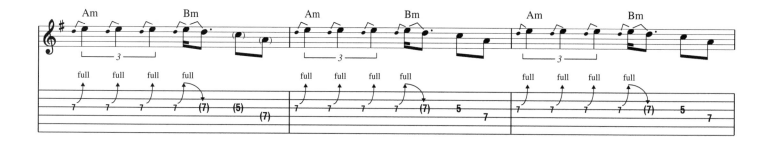

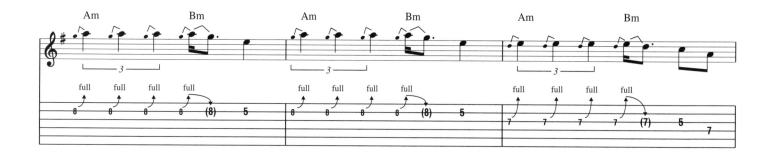

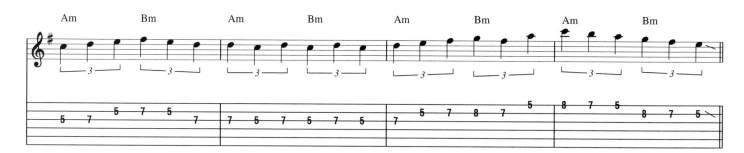

Interlude

Gtr. 1: w/ Riff A

D.S. al Coda
(take 2nd lyrics)

3. The

✆ Coda

Verse

fire. _____ Yeah. ___ 4. You know that it would be un-true. ___ You

know that I would be a li - ar,   if I was to say to you, ___

Chorus

"Girl, we could-n't get much high - er."   Come on, ba - by, light my   fire. ___

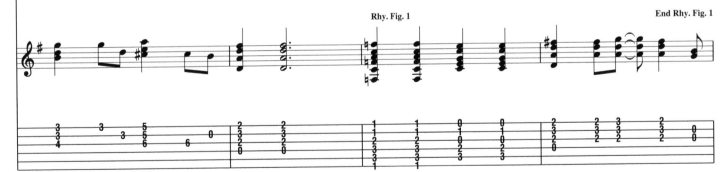

Come on ba - by, light my   fire. ___   Try to set the night on   fire. ___

Rhy. Fig. 1   **End Rhy. Fig. 1**

Gtr. 2: w/ Rhy. Fig. 1, 2 times, simile

Try to set the night on   fire. ___   Try to set the night on   fire. ___

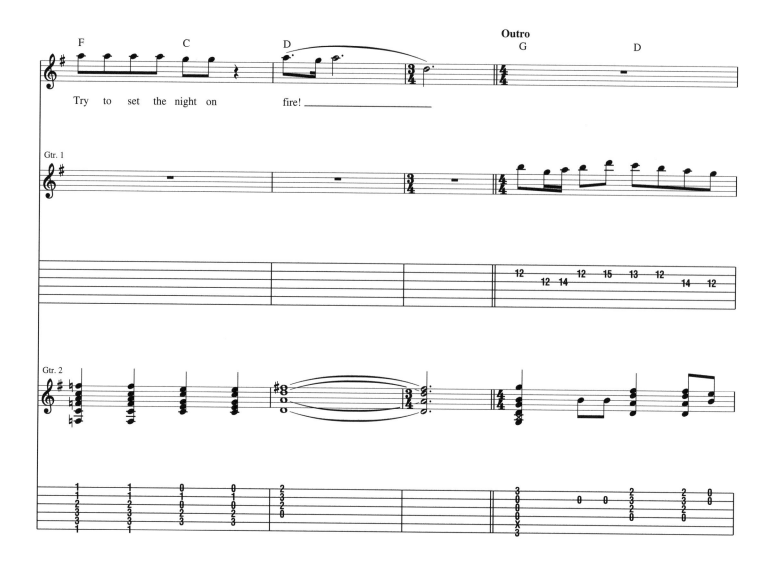

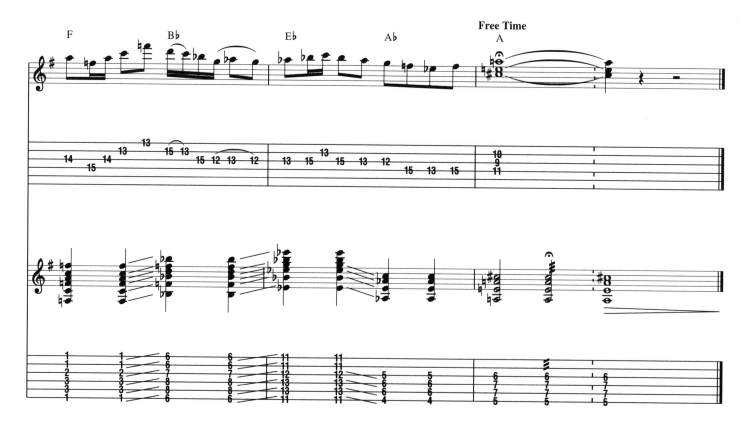

Love Her Madly

Words and Music by The Doors

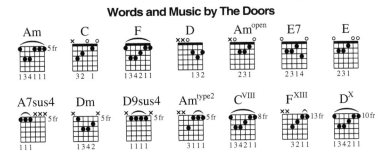

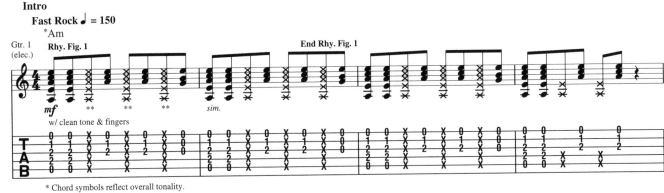

Intro

Fast Rock ♩ = 150

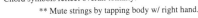

* Chord symbols reflect overall tonality.

** Mute strings by tapping body w/ right hand.

thou - sand times be - fore?___ Don't you

love her ways? ___ A, tell me what you ___ say. ___

Don't you love her as ___ she's walk - ing out ___ the door?_

Chorus

* composite arrangement

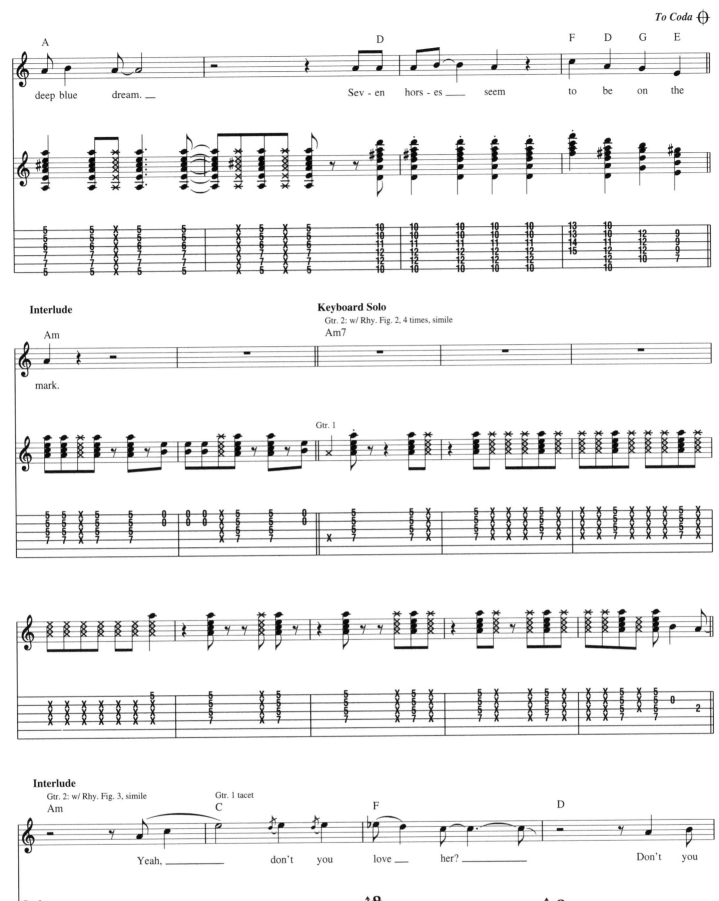

Interlude

Keyboard Solo
Gtr. 2: w/ Rhy. Fig. 2, 4 times, simile

Interlude
Gtr. 2: w/ Rhy. Fig. 3, simile

love her as _____ she's walk-ing out ____ the door? ____

Coda

Gtr. 1: w/ Rhy. Fig. 1, 2 times

Guitar Solo
Gtr. 1: w/ Rhy. Fig. 1, 2 times, simile

* Gtr. 4 tabbed to the left of slash.

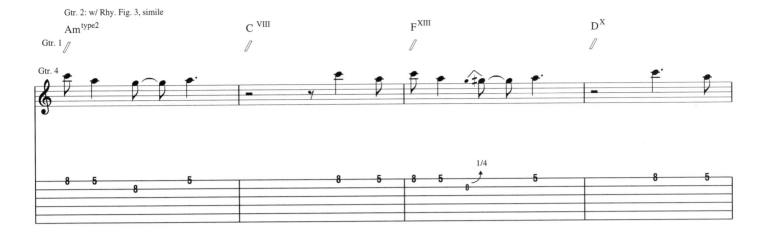

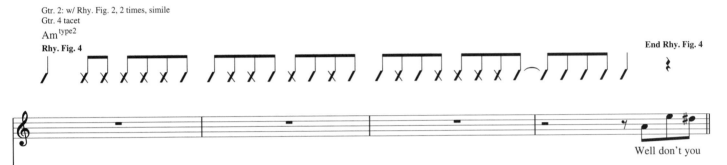

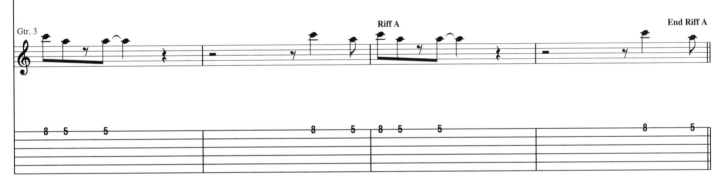

Well don't you

Outro

Gtr. 1: w/ Rhy. Fig. 4, till fade, simile
Gtr. 2: w/ Rhy. Fig. 2, till fade, simile
Gtr. 3: w/ Riff A, till fade, simile

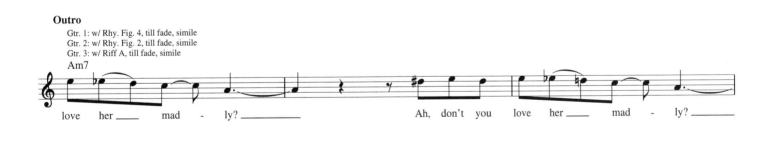

love her ___ mad - ly? ___ Ah, don't you love her ___ mad - ly? ___

___ Ah, don't you love her ___ mad - ly? ___

Love Me Two Times

Words and Music by The Doors

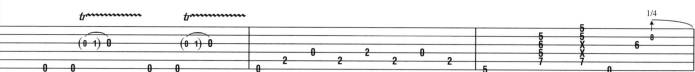

Pre-Chorus

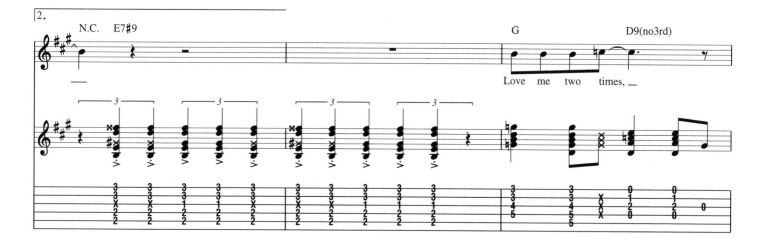

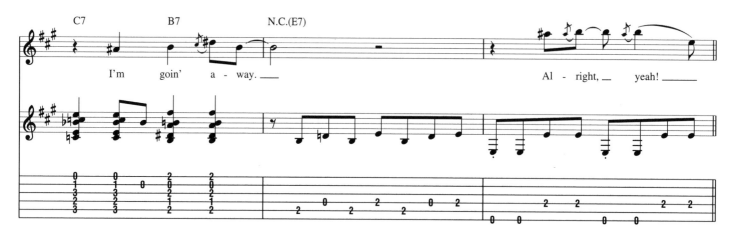

Keyboard Solo

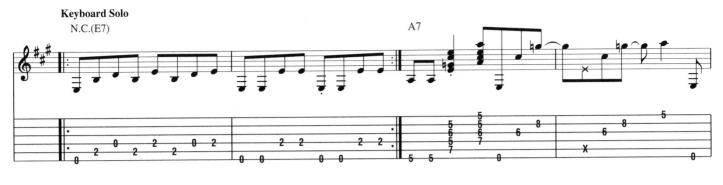

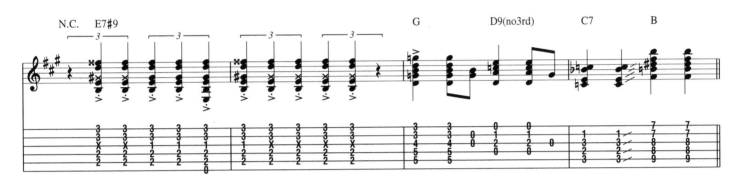

D.S. al Coda

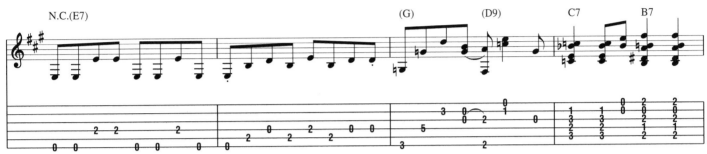

3. Love me one time, ___

Love me two times, ___   I'm gone a-way! ___

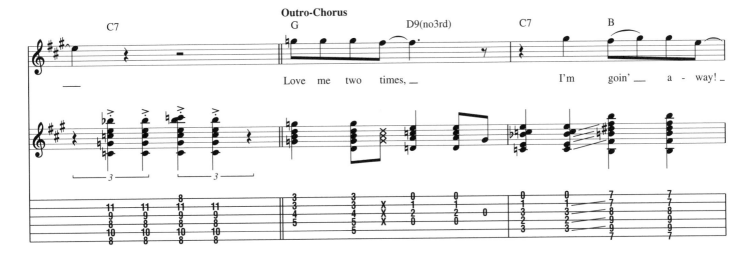

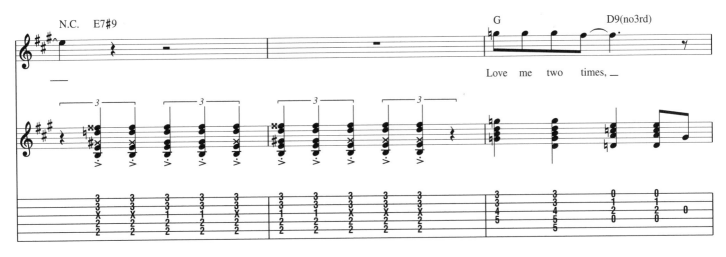

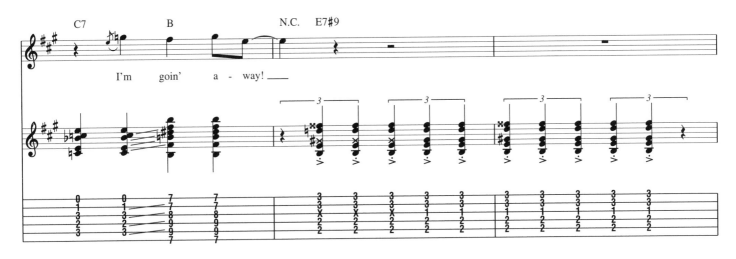

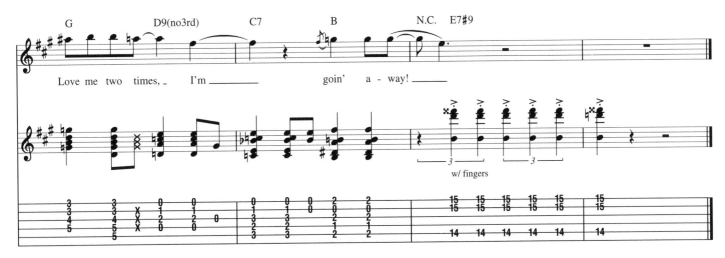

People Are Strange

Words and Music by The Doors

Chorus

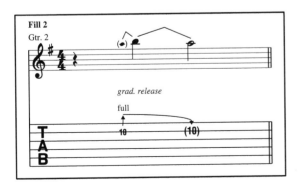

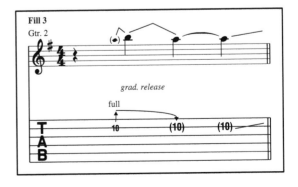

D.S. al Coda

* Played as even eighth notes.

Coda

Keyboard Solo

All - right, yeah. ___

Outro-Chorus

When you're strange, _____ fac - es come out ___ of the rain. _

When you're strange, no one re - mem - bers your name. _

When you're strange, _ when you're strange, _ when you're strange. _

Roadhouse Blues

Words and Music by The Doors

* Key signature denotes E Mixolydian.

2. Yeah in back of the road - house they got some __ bun - ga - lows. __

Yeah, in back of the road - house they

got some __ bun - ga - lows. __ And

that's for the peo - ple who like to go __ down slow. __

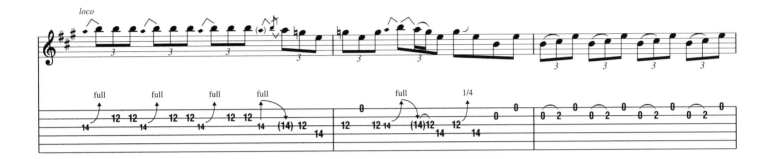

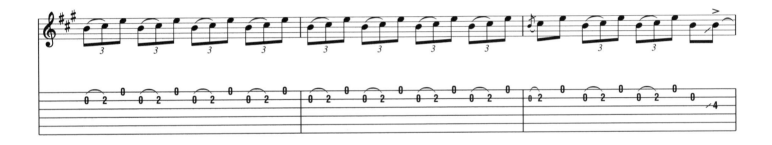

Interlude

N.C.(E7)

You got - ta roll, roll, roll, you got - ta

* nonsense syllables

Guitar Notation Legend

Guitar Music can be notated three different ways: on a *musical staff*, in *tablature*, and in *rhythm slashes*.

RHYTHM SLASHES are written above the staff. Strum chords in the rhythm indicated. Use the chord diagrams found at the top of the first page of the transcription for the appropriate chord voicings. Round noteheads indicate single notes.

THE MUSICAL STAFF shows pitches and rhythms and is divided by bar lines into measures. Pitches are named after the first seven letters of the alphabet.

TABLATURE graphically represents the guitar fingerboard. Each horizontal line represents a a string, and each number represents a fret.

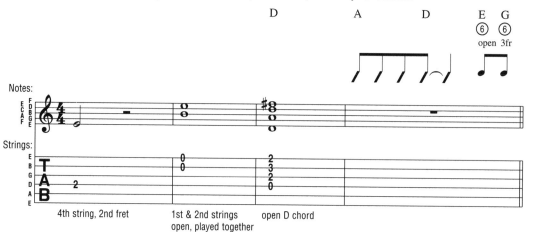

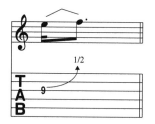

4th string, 2nd fret   1st & 2nd strings open, played together   open D chord

Definitions for Special Guitar Notation

HALF-STEP BEND: Strike the note and bend up 1/2 step.

WHOLE-STEP BEND: Strike the note and bend up one step.

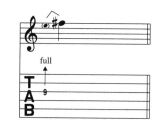

GRACE NOTE BEND: Strike the note and bend up as indicated. The first note does not take up any time.

SLIGHT (MICROTONE) BEND: Strike the note and bend up 1/4 step.

BEND AND RELEASE: Strike the note and bend up as indicated, then release back to the original note. Only the first note is struck.

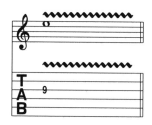

PRE-BEND: Bend the note as indicated, then strike it.

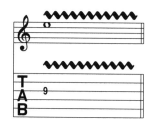

PRE-BEND AND RELEASE: Bend the note as indicated. Strike it and release the bend back to the original note.

UNISON BEND: Strike the two notes simultaneously and bend the lower note up to the pitch of the higher.

VIBRATO: The string is vibrated by rapidly bending and releasing the note with the fretting hand.

WIDE VIBRATO: The pitch is varied to a greater degree by vibrating with the fretting hand.

HAMMER-ON: Strike the first (lower) note with one finger, then sound the higher note (on the same string) with another finger by fretting it without picking.

PULL-OFF: Place both fingers on the notes to be sounded. Strike the first note and without picking, pull the finger off to sound the second (lower) note.

LEGATO SLIDE: Strike the first note and then slide the same fret-hand finger up or down to the second note. The second note is not struck.

SHIFT SLIDE: Same as legato slide, except the second note is struck.

TRILL: Very rapidly alternate between the notes indicated by continuously hammering on and pulling off.

TAPPING: Hammer ("tap") the fret indicated with the pick-hand index or middle finger and pull off to the note fretted by the fret hand.

NATURAL HARMONIC: Strike the note while the fret-hand lightly touches the string directly over the fret indicated.

Harm.

PINCH HARMONIC: The note is fretted normally and a harmonic is produced by adding the edge of the thumb or the tip of the index finger of the pick hand to the normal pick attack.

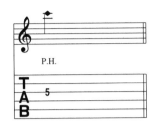

P.H.

HARP HARMONIC: The note is fretted normally and a harmonic is produced by gently resting the pick hand's index finger directly above the indicated fret (in parentheses) while the pick hand's thumb or pick assists by plucking the appropriate string.

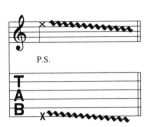

H.H.

PICK SCRAPE: The edge of the pick is rubbed down (or up) the string, producing a scratchy sound.

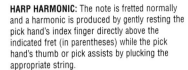

P.S.

MUFFLED STRINGS: A percussive sound is produced by laying the fret hand across the string(s) without depressing, and striking them with the pick hand.

PALM MUTING: The note is partially muted by the pick hand lightly touching the string(s) just before the bridge.

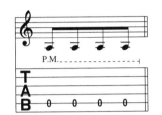

P.M.

RAKE: Drag the pick across the strings indicated with a single motion.

rake

TREMOLO PICKING: The note is picked as rapidly and continuously as possible.

ARPEGGIATE: Play the notes of the chord indicated by quickly rolling them from bottom to top.

VIBRATO BAR DIVE AND RETURN: The pitch of the note or chord is dropped a specified number of steps (in rhythm) then returned to the original pitch.

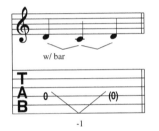

w/ bar

-1

VIBRATO BAR SCOOP: Depress the bar just before striking the note, then quickly release the bar.

w/ bar

VIBRATO BAR DIP: Strike the note and then immediately drop a specified number of steps, then release back to the original pitch.

w/ bar

Additional Musical Definitions

(accent)	• Accentuate note (play it louder)	

Rhy. Fig.   • Label used to recall a recurring accompaniment pattern (usually chordal).

(accent)   • Accentuate note with great intensity

Riff   • Label used to recall composed, melodic lines (usually single notes) which recur.

(staccato)   • Play the note short

Fill   • Label used to identify a brief melodic figure which is to be inserted into the arrangement.

⊓   • Downstroke

Rhy. Fill   • A chordal version of a Fill.

∨   • Upstroke

tacet   • Instrument is silent (drops out).

D.S. al Coda   • Go back to the sign (𝄋), then play until the measure marked "***To Coda***," then skip to the section labelled "***Coda***."

D.S. al Fine   • Go back to the beginning of the song and play until the measure marked "***Fine***" (end).

• Repeat measures between signs.

1. 2.

• When a repeated section has different endings, play the first ending only the first time and the second ending only the second time.

NOTE: Tablature numbers in parentheses mean:
1. The note is being sustained over a system (note in standard notation is tied), or
2. The note is sustained, but a new articulation (such as a hammer-on, pull-off, slide or vibrato begins, or
3. The note is a barely audible "ghost" note (note in standard notation is also in parentheses).